DANIEL LEE

Faith Not Fear

Copyright © 2020 by Daniel Lee

All rights reserved. No part of this publication may be reproduced, distributed, or transmitted in any form or by any means, including photocopying, recording, or other electronic or mechanical methods, without the prior written permission of the publisher, except in the case of brief quotations embodied in critical reviews and certain other noncommercial uses permitted by copyright law.

ISBN: 978-1-7355552-1-8

First Edition: December 2020

Printed in the United States of America

www.iamdaniellee.com

Dedication

I want to take this time to dedicate this book, "Faith Not Fear," to my wife LaToya Sharee. She was there to push me in getting what was inside out in ways I would have never pursued on my own. Most times, your help came indirectly. And those inadvertent encounters caused me to record on paper what was buried deep inside of my heart, only for me to share with you today how I was able to recover lost hope and redeeming confidence through faith from fear.

So I say, Thank you for believing in me when I didn't think to give myself a chance to believe in my ability to be a successful author. Thank you for personally challenging me by the examples you've inadvertently set before me. Thank you for allowing yourself to be led by the Holy Spirit through suggestive hints, your watchfulness, and your patience.

Therefore, I acknowledge that I am alive and well in spirit because of having a friend like you. Your hand in my life has never been taken for granted, and I appreciate your labor of love by your examples of truth toward me every day.

Table of Contents

Introduction 1
Chapter 1: Hidden Figures 4
Chapter 2: Controlling Limitations 7
Chapter 3: Distractions 11
Chapter 4: Knock, Knock..14
Chapter 5: Difference Makers 23
Chapter 6: Faith That Stretches Your Strength.............32
Chapter 7: The Faith Cycle..36
Chapter 8: When It's Your Turn 40
Chapter 9: The Process of Faith..................................44
Chapter 10: Expectancy...48
Chapter 11: Repent, Release & Repeat 51
Chapter 12: Wandering in the Past is a Trap...............55
Citations..57
Biblical References..58
About the Author..61

Introduction

This subject will shed light on why it is essential to living a life full of applicable Faith every day! You will begin to see what fear does and how Faith subdues the sting of such an infant emotion. This book Faith Not Fear was written for all who realize what they do and the importance of trusting oneself, controlling limitations, distractions, and helps every reader have confidence in his daily activities.

In the cause of reading this book, you will remember why you were chosen of GOD and that you know for assurance that you are more than conquerors through Christ Jesus who strengthens you! You have been encouraged in this book to take your rightful position back as Kings of men within the Kingdom of GOD and OWN the declarations you've spoken over your life. Faith Not Fear was written to help you dethrone and dispose of all negative aspects and dispositions of fears you may face in life.

God's promises are revealed to you by consistently seeking the truth of who you are through GOD's word. Follow through on purpose by walking in the fullness of God's spoken victory over your life and say goodbye to every distraction that suggests otherwise.

I want to take you down a journey that is not meant for the faint at heart. I wouldn't want to know how your opinion is formed about me after this read. When it is your turn to follow through on what it is to truly follow the call for responsive obedience, you'll have to make decisions that are unpopular to the world's standards. Let your decision be made known as I have. I will not cower away nor crawl under a rock in retribution of disgrace because of the fear of people's opinions here on Earth.

El-Shaddai is My Rock, My Source, and Shield!

This is the declaration I recite whenever I need to be inspired. At the end of this book, I'll share why it is important to speak declarations over yourself, your family, purpose, vision, and future.

Adonai El Roi (The Lord is my Shepherd) is My Judge. He sees me as I am sheltered and handsome in His sight. I know HIS Voice, and I shall only answer the call to HIS Voice alone. My life is in His hands. My heart belongs to Him. I agree with the purpose of His blood He shed for me. Therefore, I Live by Faith and fear has and will be forever dismissed in the Name of Yeshua forever! Amen.

See scriptures below:

Psalm 23:1-6 (NIV)

"The LORD is my shepherd, I lack nothing. He makes me lie down in green pastures, He leads me beside quiet waters, He refreshes my soul. He guides me along the right paths for His name's sake. Even though I walk through the darkest valley, I will fear no evil, for YOU are with me; YOUR rod and YOUR staff, they comfort me. YOU prepare a table before me in the presence of my enemies. YOU anoint my head with oil; my cup overflows. Surely YOUR goodness and love will follow me all the days of my life, and I will dwell in the house of the LORD forever."

2 TIMOTHY 1:7 AMP

"For GOD did not give us a spirit of timidity or cowardice or fear, but [He has given us a spirit] of power and of love and of sound judgment and personal discipline [abilities that result in a calm, well-balanced mind and self-control]."

Chapter 1
Hidden Figures

As men and women of the Most High, we should not hide behind who we truly believe in because of what is currently in front of our path. Nor should we be afraid or mentally preoccupied with things that arise before us because these things may cause us to doubt getting through such obstacles. Our focus should be on Christ and Christ alone! To trust Christ is to be free and freedom is the transformation of the mind.

Whenever you find yourself dealing with disbelief, doubt, and fear of a given situation or circumstance, we unknowingly create a crisis of belief. Henry Blackaby said, *"A <u>crisis of belief</u> is when GOD gives us an assignment that we cannot do on our own. Some people* *may decide not to do the assignment because they believe that the task is impossible. This is the crisis of belief."*

When we remove our limitations off of ourselves and give reverence to Him who gives us strength and confidence to do everything, anything is achievable. I rest on this biblical statement in Philippians 14:13, where it reads, "I can do all things through Christ that strengthens me." Thus, you've got to replace the "WHAT" you know with the "WHO" you know and look toward having weights you've been carrying by your strength onto the shoulders of Him who has all power to promote unto you the peace you need to make it through.

Do not question His character, power, presence, or authority in your life! It is written in John 14:6, where Christ said, "I am the way, the truth, and the life." We are to let go of figuring out how things will work out and solely trust in Him to work it all out. There will come a time when you will realize, just as it says in Romans 8:28, "and we know [with great confidence] that God [who is deeply concerned about us] causes all things to work together [as a plan] for good for those who love God, to those who are called according to His plan and purpose."

Here's the issue, we as humans want to control everything and manage every detail until completion without letting go of prior pains or emotional baggage. Such is not the way, and that's not how true faith works for a nation of believers.

Q: What happens when you find in your journey that you've asked and sought GOD for something, He provides the way, and you then begin to move in it and afterward, recognize challenges are forming along the way?

A: Continue to trust in Him while digging a little deeper in your faith so that He could prove that it is only He who gives the victory. *1 Corinthians 15:57 "But thanks be to GOD, who gives us the victory through our Lord Messiah YESHUA."*

Chapter 2
Controlling Limitations

The issues we as people have regarding basic principles of our trust with GOD are contingent on how much we control things to believe that GOD will do what He says. It's like we won't fully believe in His Words because of the impossibility of our finite mode of thinking. This is the same reference I pointed to earlier in the last chapter on the Crisis of Belief. However, the crisis seems like we'll wait until we see something happen before our eyes, the things we need before we believe what GOD said is true. But my question is, WHY? Is it the fear of being denied or even looking crazy to others because of a decision we made to trust GOD isn't popular to society? Or is it that we don't know what true faith is, how to use it, or even how to trust GOD in general?

James 2:26 reads, "For as the body without the spirit is dead, so faith without works is dead also."

I've learned that having 100% faith in who GOD is, meant that GOD's heart is full of joy because of my acts of faith in choosing my heart to use His wisdom instead of my own (Proverbs 23:15-16). One breakthrough I've learned was to make everything about the Word of God as personal as possible. How did I do that? Making the scriptures personal and practical allowed me to see that GOD is speaking to me directly in my situation. The impact is so much greater.

I'll give you an example, For GOD so loved the world (inserted my name here), that He gave his only begotten son, that when (I) believed in him, would not perish but that (I) may have everlasting life...

When you take the Word practically and intimately, you make it impossible for the Word of GOD to fail within your heart because you meant its application wholeheartedly. Therefore, make every attempt to remember that it is He that gives you the power to rest in His Word and to believe in His Might, His Authority, and His Amazing Spirit. Doing so removes your limitations and takes the burden of responsibility off your shoulders so that GOD himself, within His perfect timing, accomplishes His will in you the way He originally intended.

I am also reminded of *Ephesians 3:20 (NIV): "Now to Him who is able to do immeasurably more than all we ask or imagine, according to his power that is at work within us."*

This passage is a tremendous help to reassure that He has everything held together in His hands. Before we get to the promises GOD has arranged for us, it is good we learn what He's trying to teach us.

Moses and the Israelites roamed and wandered in the wilderness for 40 years. Generally, because they were inconsistent with their faith and obedience to His word, they had difficulties letting go of their past mental slavery conditions. Their journey from bondage to the Promised Land should have taken them eleven days instead of forty years to acquire their inheritance. At that, the entire Moses/Israelite generation had to live out their life, roaming around in the wilderness before ever getting what was promised to them due to lack of obedience. However, because GOD is faithful and His word will never return to Him void, He raised yet another leader that would diligently lead the following generation into the Promised Land.

As you follow GOD's leading, be sure that you are obedient through each encounter. This is so that you may mature with each lesson and reach the promises designed specifically for you during your lifetime here on Earth as a Kingdom citizen. But also, make sure that your heart's posture is in right standing, without error or wrong motives. Continuously ask the Holy Spirit to create in you a clean heart, to purify you, that you are to be cleansed with hyssop through and through.

What GOD has for you is for you, and your inheritances shall be passed down from generation to generation.

Chapter 3
Distractions

1 Corinthians 10:13 AMP

No temptation [regardless of its source] has overtaken or enticed you that is not common to human experience [nor is any temptation unusual or beyond human resistance]; but GOD is faithful [to His word—He is compassionate and trustworthy], and He will not let you be tempted beyond your ability [to resist], but along with the temptation He [has in the past and is now and] will [always] provide the way out as well, so that you will be able to endure it [without yielding, and will overcome temptation with joy].

If we are not careful in WHOM we believe, we will

often be left wide open and available for anything to creep in and distract us from living out our divine truth in Him. One thing about the adversary is that he'll use the smallest issues he knows that bother or annoy us. As being connected on this Earth, we humans cause unwanted attention to ourselves by openly complaining or grumbling over things, leaving the atmosphere wide open and uncovered for anything to latch on. Therefore, the enemy has open rights to attach a device or a buffet to the persuasion of lies or anything opposite of what GOD said, to get us thinking less of ourselves. Please remember that the thief only comes to steal, kill, and destroy. Ultimately, those things shift us into doubting GOD's word over our lives and cause us to forget about His promises. Need I say, Distractions!

Even to the point where the enemy will try to get us to doubt how real and alive GOD's presence is within us. Due to us not staying focused, this type of device is meant to be a distraction. The very simplest issue eventually becomes louder than the voice of GOD. It unknowingly makes that simplistic issue an idol because we allowed it to focus on how we solve the problem instead of focusing on WHO is placed in our heart ahead of the solution.

It only takes one paper cut, one small chink in the armor, for the enemy to find your unprotected, vulnerable area, inflicting pain and suffering, frustrations, and confusion. However, if left unchecked, that infliction may easily turn into an infection.

Naturally, infections are those invading microorganisms of bacteria, fungal viruses, and unwanted parasites that multiply and spread to other areas in the body. In some cases, infectious bacteria may give off toxins, which can be more severe in the body. These are true statements in the natural sense, so in the spirit as well. These are simple laws on how infectious diseases operate. Untreated cuts, sores, wounds, and even careless sensual activity may very well lead to disaster. How you treat yourself in spirit may operate the same way. Have you been spiritually protected from outside harm and danger to the maturity of your spiritual growth? Are you haphazardly living out each day as if your life in the spirit realm does not need to be examined closely? My friends, this is important.

If you are distracted by things and people to the point where your focus is off GOD's word, you've just placed that thing or person before GOD. I purposefully paint the picture this way because it is that extreme. However, we must make sure we know what our priorities are and what a distraction is. Distinguish your main objectives, needs, wants, and desires in a posture prioritized in the order by which GOD provides details of how to manage all those things.

You must remain covered, grounded, secured, and always focused on GOD's loving hedge of protection. By

FAITH, seek to remain covered by His grace.

Chapter 4
Knock, Knock

In this chapter, I will be 100% transparent to my readers. The objective is to invite you into some of the challenges I faced as I recall trying times in my struggles with faith and ultimately living with fear.

It was the little faith I had in trusting GOD's word over my life that I had to decide to vacate the abnormal life I thought was comfortable. I was talented but comfortable, not in my creativity. Gifted in prophetic mime dance interpretation but comfortable not cultivating that gift for others to experience. Anointed in the ministry to build and teach like-minded individuals but comfortable with not being stretched to teach; comfortable being tied to an unequally yoked marriage.

For three years, I held the status of being a married man as an honored accomplishment as I should, but I guess back then, I held that position with a lesser degree of godly structure of more importance. I thought all I had to do was remain an honest man, raise my son in the best way I could and figure everything else out as they came along with no clear direction. I had no real vision or a plan in leading my family like a godly man should have. I lacked family leadership as a man. My identity was lost in translation, and I didn't even realize it.

There were other issues with me figuring out how to balance my real purpose, marriage life, fatherhood, and understanding life as a leader and teacher of the gifts I was given. I participated in the church here and there and still ran away from a calling I received years ago. I never considered that my name would one day be called to serve beyond my comfort level of serving because I made up in my heart of excuses that I wasn't ready. I knew my life as I lived wasn't worth taking the credit for that type of responsibility all in all.

In twelve years, I've made some foolish decisions and those decisions, even though I knew they weren't upstanding as a Christian man of God, were questionable at best. I allowed myself to woefully gain hypocrite tendencies. I had given into frequently drinking alcohol and smoking black and milds, and my excuses for using those substances were attempts to mellow out social drama and low self-esteem.

In my past marriage, I was the one who was the problem solver, the one who communicated on every issue out of the two of us, but we still had communication problems. Problems that I thought I could solve in my strength and in my way. Several times through friendship to marriage, I managed to change up communication styles to be heard. But of course, every attempt failed because I didn't acknowledge GOD enough to steer the ship.

The three-year marriage stint felt more like bondage of barriers than a partnership of growth and focus, mixed with immoral compromises of disillusioned responsibilities, moral decay for hard-working togetherness, and relational non-problem solving capabilities. I sometimes had to turn blue in the face to get her to come to attend church services with our one-year-old son and me. However, because I permitted dysfunction for so long, those problems became harder to criticize the necessary changes needed to survive the already damaged marriage.

My mindset was geared to solving other people's problems and pacifying our spiritual health and well being as a family to what made her happy. There was nothing wrong with giving my wife what she wanted. However, my giving came at an expense where the term "happy wife, happy life" was extreme because that sacrifice allowed me to compromise my spiritual foundation. That was my entire fault. For years, I have dealt with the fear of being rejected, and I surely didn't want to be rejected in my marriage as it came to doing things together as one unit. Immaturity led me to form habits or behaviors that would allow me to base my decisions on if my family could participate as a unit, then I wouldn't pursue what was essentially right from an inclusion standpoint. It was there that I allowed what I thought I wanted to become to be louder than what I knew was best. I went from church to church, trying not to be used in the capacity I once started in my youthful zeal for the Lord.

After a while, I refused to search for my purpose and ultimately diminished using my gift but still wanted to be considered a man of GOD's own heart. HOW? I knew what I needed to do, how I was to live, and what it would take to live a righteous lifestyle for my family, and everybody had to be on board with these changes. Something in me noticed that I was living an oxymoronic lifestyle and that conviction led me to know there would be a fight on the horizon to transition into righteousness across the board.

Then, something shifted. In a state of desperation, I stemmed from not getting any of my prayers heard from heaven. I found my back up against walls of defending myself, not being heard in marriage from my spouse without probable cause, and seemingly losing the grip of my self-worth in the process. I must have prayed the right prayer and gained access to ask the right question to GOD. Shortly after, my life took a turn. I was introduced to a local family church and a separate online bible study group through Facebook. They became the tools I needed in establishing a deeper connection with the Lord through intentional and consistent studying of the word of God.

I had to look at myself through the lens of God's word to exactly see what was defective in my life and the view of me trying to use God into giving me tangible things without genuinely surrendering wholeheartedly. In the nightly online bible study, we were led to study Proverbs and Ephesians. This is the part I heard the Holy Spirit and the voice of the spirit of wisdom KNOCK on the gates of my heart, louder than I have ever. What aided the furtherance of awakening within were DAILY chapter homework questions. The structured questions were geared to challenge me traditionally, apply what I believed, and represent important tools to hold me accountable to what was learned.

Publicly posting my homework became joyous as I read and related to others' homework and testimonies of life-changing events in their lives. That meant that I was not alone in seeking Kingdom truths re-establishing my relationship with the Lord. Those experiences gave me new confidences I hadn't felt in years. I found it compelling to worship God through obediently remaining consistent in seeking out real spiritual truths for that time in my life. I knew that I wanted God to heal the holes in my relationship with Him and all the craters of doubt I took hold of, imploding factors of low self-esteem, false characteristics I formed. Those were all the inner struggles I faced as I looked in the mirror of who I had become. However, I knew change was on the horizon. I was excited about the Word of God again. I began sharing the good news with my spouse at the time and was often disappointed with her disdain for wanting to learn and grow as a family. I always wondered why I have to figuratively pull her arm to have her join me in spiritual events that were designed to improve our lives. She just wasn't interested in living right. Living righteously to her, I guess it was too boring, too safe, and no fun. All I could find rebuttal in my heart during those times were Psalm 34:8, "O taste and see that the Lord [our God] is good." However, I would often pray that God reveals what I should do about this.

Things began to happen supernaturally, and before I knew it, after a series of uncooperative events with my spouse, I became a divorced man and father of two young boys. I was attacked over and over and over again. Some days, the attacks seemed like they'd never let up; so much pressure from the enemy, disguised through my ex-wife, a relentless attack of my character. What made matters worse was her selfish and narcissistic emotions because I was shut out from seeing my children.

It was the most emotionally draining and painful event I've ever encountered. I never thought being raised with my father outside of the home would happen to my children like I had to experience as a young man. However, I knew everything was in GOD's hands. The decisions I've made to get to a place of discovery made no sense. I thought I was selfish with my growth without them, but I had to remain faithful to GOD, knowing that my life was in His hands, I had to release my control. I purged, fasted, prayed, forgave, and I kept stepping forward through all the pain because I knew it would get better.

There will come a time when you have to sacrifice your own will and control of things in your life to build GOD's trust again. You will have to endure many unpopular challenges to society and other GOD-led decisions that will seem questionable to others. The key is to follow the direction God is showing you. He will reveal His truth to you through His word, through His messengers, and other various confirmations required to keep you arranged on the right path. The journey will not be easy. But if you really want to be aligned in what the desires of GOD's heart is designed for you, then you cannot fear what you cannot control. Your experience may not be as extreme as mine. However, you will need to let go and let GOD be GOD in all of your affairs. He knows best, just like He did with the three Hebrew boys in the furnace and Daniel in the lion's den, and Joseph while in prison because of wrongful persecution. Our dependence on GOD is our life! Faith Is A LIFESTYLE Meant Living and true faith involves action.

There were many days I cried, battling with overwhelming emotions and fear. I was discouraged because of the fear of failing my boys, absenteeism, tremendous clouds of doubt, thoughts of not making it through, revolving cycles of worrying, and confusion at times. But I always knew to run to my retreat of worship music on Spotify, catching mini-sermons on Facebook and YouTube, which helped confirm the word I would receive from studying to get me through those trails of darkness.

Along the way, the revelation came as a result of frequently making faith-based decisions and being obedient in the changing of my mindset. I realized that my emotions acted as blinders, and the fear I gave into were literal earplugs to the spiritual frequency of GOD's voice. It was time for me to fully remove what I could not control and let go to receive a breakthrough. So, I positioned my heart and everything I thought of in giving it all over to GOD to carry. Here is where I discovered that my faith became the ultimate peace source and not just a feeling.

Matthew 11:28-30

"Come unto me, all ye that labour and are heavy laden, and I will give you rest. Take my yoke upon you, and learn of me; for I am meek and lowly in heart: and ye shall find rest unto your souls. For my yoke is easy, and my burden is light."

I faced my fears by taking off every burden from my shoulders and giving GOD my broken heart, all of my fears and failures. I made sure I intentionally invited Him into all of my decisions, study efforts, and everything. I mustered up the little faith I had to move what I thought was a mountain before me. The mountain was the limitations I set on myself through negative criticism.

After learning how to constantly move out of the way, I felt the gates of Heaven's Kingdom welcoming my every move. I began to walk in purpose and learned to consistently denounce every negative murmur I heard, seconds before they could settle in my heart. I finally discovered the life of what walking by faith felt like. Although I wasn't out of the woods yet, and because I already know how complacency plotted me in a spiraling life-altering position, I would not, on any occasion, become complacent in my heart ever again into thinking I have arrived.

You must examine your life's direction by consulting with the Holy Spirit, in making your life's calling *"an election sure" (2 Peter 10)*. Nevertheless, there is always something to learn, improve, and mature every day. Take nothing, and I mean nothing, for granted. Serve each other like you want to be treated and give your time to one another when you see a need or someone to help. Be led by the Holy Spirit!

Chapter 5
Difference Makers

As we confess and believe that Christ was raised from the dead, we are saved according to Romans 10:9.

So there also comes a transition or a shift in the way we are now considered to believe.

What does it mean to believe?

To believe is to accept something as true; to feel sure of, to acknowledge the truth of...

Believe in who you are as you discover new areas in your walk with Christ as you never have on a level like this before.

I want to challenge you to make a declaration of who you are and what you want out of life, where you could impact the world, using the gifts and talents GOD has given.

If you are unaware or unsure, just ask the Holy Spirit for guidance.

Once you have done so, be intentional about taking strides to accomplish your declarations as they manifest in your life.

We are not meant to be a part of this world but to be set apart, to be the difference makers in righteousness.

"And do not be conformed to this world [any longer with its superficial values and customs], but be transformed and progressively changed [as you mature spiritually] by the renewing of your mind [focusing on Godly values and ethical attitudes], so that you may prove [for yourselves] what the will of God is, that which is good and acceptable and perfect [in His plan and purpose for you]."

ROMANS 12:2 AMP.

We have now been given all spiritual gifts from God, our Father, and with the amazing help of The Holy Spirit, that NOTHING is impossible.

Create yourself a new outlook on your life within.

I want to share a story with you regarding Jesus, Peter, and the rest of his disciples and reasons why it's important not to lose hope or faith. In the book of Matthew 14:22-32, the story talks about when Jesus sent His disciples to travel ahead of Him (concern #1) in a boat after feeding a crowd of about five thousand people. Shortly before dawn, Jesus went out to them, walking on the sea. The disciples knew they were far off from where they came from and knew that Jesus was not on the boat with them before they left. Some time passed, and they began to see a figure come toward them in the midst of what seemed to be for the rough seas. Out of the wind-bordered sea, the disciple began to panic, thinking that the figure they saw was a ghost. However, as the figure drew closer, they saw that it was Jesus, and they still doubted. They immediately concluded that no man could defy gravity and walk on water, much less with unfavorable weather. 1) How come they didn't immediately consider that it was Jesus they saw as a figure out on the water?

The disciples already knew that He was not with them as they departed town. I imagine that they probably never got any rest because of over-thinking, "How will Jesus meet with us on the other side if He's not here riding with us?" [Aha! fearpoint#1]

If you know you've been given an assignment, led by God, is there a way to know that you've already been equipped to handle whatever tasks that come along?

Is the concern for who comes along with you during your assignment a focal point? No, it should not be. Who comes along is not your concern. God equips, and God provides.

Even if you had a team of your trusted advisors, you still are required to lean on the guidance of the Holy Spirit to lead you through all things. Not all experiences you face will be followed up with your learned expertise on making decisions on a dime. However, discernment and wisdom should always be readily available.

Back to the story,

Once Jesus called out to them and told them it was Him, Peter (the only one who had a bold and conscious thought) asked, "IF it is really you, tell me to come out and walk to you." When Peter received the command to come, he got out of the boat and began stepping on top of the water, walking toward Jesus.

I imagine that he was excited and confident that he achieved the impossible by walking over the top of deep water without a platform—just his faith. However, because of the conditions of the wind and waves, it frightened him. Peter began to sink. Jesus then immediately grabbed hold of him. At this point, I imagined Jesus asked Peter, why did you doubt and allow yourself to be diverted from concentrating on me? I needed you to learn how to depend on me, even when the issues of Life seem unattainable. Wow!

Waiting for your breakthrough, promise, and victory is contingent on what's going on in your mind. So, what are you focusing on?

I have a peculiar imagination, so I thought that because the disciples knew that He sent them on a boat without His presence, they worried. I even think they worried so much that they didn't get any sleep throughout the night until the morning. He approached the boat on the water. They probably could not understand why Jesus decided not to roll with them this time.

Even though you are used to things going the way they normally would, that does not mean that they will continue to follow or yield the same processes as before. When God is ready to do something different in your life, you must first be sensitive enough to notice whenever He's made a change. Second, you must know that change is for you to seek Him for the direction He wants you to go. For instance, I noticed that I began to feel uneasy. That is because the Holy Spirit was trying to usher me to pour out on paper what was being downloaded from Heaven.

{God will give you a daily schedule}, filled with things to do supernaturally and systematically! For me, those things were discussion topics to include in this book, details of how to explain the revelation of it, how it correlates to His word, and how to help it make sense so that my vision will help encourage others to do the same. Glory to HIS Name Forever! I felt that one...

🔑 The key to the victory of obedience is to understand what God wants you to do each day and then follow through with it on purpose. Don't stop until you have completed those tasks. Allow me to let you in on a secret.... He's already given you the strength to perform each task, and AS YOU DO, HE STRENGTHENS EVEN MORE!!! Yes, I have felt the difference each time. I tell you the truth.

"For I know the plans I have for you," declares the Lord, "plans to prosper you and not to harm you, plans to give you hope and a future."

Jeremiah 29:11 NIV

He exactly knows what He wants for you. We often think we know what we want and need, but we have no clue what is even necessary for our need to grow.

They were getting used to being with Jesus step by step. You know how you have a best friend or someone you don't want to let go of.

Pain helps your relationships in ways that will allow truth to work out your issues rather than allowing the truth to hurt you.

GOD will show us the history of who we are in Him before walking in total victory. Only through Christ do we have complete victory. That is to remain strong, steadfast, and unmovable because of the power and authority that rests in us. It is not by might, nor by power that we operate our own, but because we abide in Christ and actively apply God's word, we will constantly be supplied everything we need through His spirit.

We stand in truth when we are obedient to trust in the Kingdom systems of His ways even though we may not fully comprehend. For some, this display of belief was not an abiding trust of true faith in YESHUA as Savior, Lord, Provider, Protector, Friend, Beginning and End, Healer, Lawyer, Judge, Jury, Source, Shield & Strength.

So, I ask you once more, who is GOD to you?

Is He merely a temporary someone to trust in when you get in trouble?

Is your belief based on the excitement caused by witnessing testimony of the miracles He's done for others?

If so, that's cool. However, do you want to know GOD intimately and for yourself through and through?

Change your mindset from superficial ways of thinking about him.

We've been conditioned to think that we don't have to

go through anything too compromising to experience GOD's fullness. In some instances, some don't, but many do according to the assignment level GOD has over your life. Look at the significance of how after Moses died, Joshua was next to lead GOD's people into the Promised Land. Not only was he able to do it, but GOD was always with them and sent messengers to equip "The Leader WITHIN" Joshua and the Israelites camp into building prominent characteristics of strength and courage. They would need it because GOD would give them strategies to defeat multiple enemies throughout many lands and territories to stake claim over. The victories (yes, plural) came with their own set of challenges over several years. The Israelites showed that they were willing and obedient vessels, witnessing to us in our present time.

GOD Loves those who diligently seek after Him and works all things together for good who love Him and are called according to His planned purpose. It's all about GOD's Mighty Purpose for each of us, not our fear.

"For GOD did not give us a spirit of timidity (of cowardice, of craven and cringing and fawning fear), but [He has given us a spirit] of power and of love and of calm and well-balanced mind and discipline and self-control."

2 Timothy 1:7 AMPC

True faith places you in a position to wait on the Lord. This posture of waiting describes allowing GOD to come in and set up your victories and for us not to attempt to jump into the mix with our plans or solutions.

For example, GOD told Joshua that he'd now be His vessel to lead the Israelites to the Promised Land shortly after Moses died. GOD does not need us to do anything for Him by getting ready; however, He uses us to accomplish such assignments here on Earth. The instructions GOD gave Israelites through Joshua were platforms of the many victories against all that were in opposition to them.

In the beginning chapters of Joshua, I imagine the tasks were very challenging. However, GOD knew how they would get the job done because He had already declared the victory. They were constantly found in a position to have their faith in GOD tested and stretched. Not that they didn't believe Him, but that they had to remain steadfast in His word and not be persuaded by their desires to do otherwise.

Chapter 6
Faith That Stretches Your Strength

Here's where GOD uses your faith to build you and ready you for advanced spiritual maturity.

I am reminded of the Bible passage in Luke 5, where the story talks about Yeshua seeing a few boats in the lake. He then boarded one of the boats and began teaching. Shortly after sharing the news, He told Simon to go out to the deep and cast their nets. Simon shared his concern about laboring all night and having caught nothing but did as the Lord suggested. Once they let down their nets, they needed to call in others and their boats to help retrieve the multitude of fish in their nets. The harvest was so great that their boats almost sank with the weight of fish they caught.

This story's point is that you may want to be doing things in your strength, ability, and knowledge. Still, with the guidance of His word, your faith will be tested to precede in procedures you never thought would work and will prove to be the greatest form of obedience you can exercise. We would have had our faith stretched in this right because the methods advised against what would normally be done. For Simon Peter, that day was like stretching his faith in Yeshua's word, announcing a trade of His own abilities for His planned purpose; thus, becoming one of our founding Disciples of faith.

"But you are a chosen people, a royal priesthood, a holy nation, GOD's special possession, that you may declare the praises of him who called you out of darkness into his wonderful light."

1 Peter 2:9 NIV

We must know and remember who we are in God's eyes as we celebrate our gifts, talents, skills, and abilities through the strengths He has given us. Our reward comes from how we consistently reverence our hearts posture to His purposes. Furthermore, our reward does not come from our expectation to receive, but to give and share with others in the world that they can trade themselves to follow after Christ's light.

What a wonderful and amazing gift to be called His special possession! That's some real honesty to GOD, tried and true, set "apartness" we must mean to GOD for us to be placed in a ranking of that magnitude. Only GOD's trust through Yeshua can be utilized in this kind of consecration to do special deeds according to what He wants to be done. One could never know that you are just that in truth other than merely skimming over those profound words in the bible.

My question is, how hungry are you to find God where you are and not try to wait to get cleaned up before yielding your usefulness to Him?

Most people ask God to "Use me, Lord, Use Me" but fail to follow through on the simplest test to be guided to act. Maybe because we as Christians or believers mean very well but misuse our intentions to carry out the prayer PRACTICALLY; forgetting that practical application makes our intentions become our very nature in How we follow Who we serve!! No second-guessing or any alternate plans; just straight obedience, that Now Faith. Now Faith is what God recognizes; it is not for faint-hearted believers. He is serious and has always been patient enough for His people to fully yield to His call. Get into the habit of changing your perspective of thinking you know how to get through and only lean on GOD's faith.

I had to fully be His and walk upright as if I transferred my heart for His heart. I had to go through the process of seriously denouncing anything that was not magnifying His name or purposes. This kind of life requires you to place the full weight of your being on the staff of GOD's will over your life. In this place, you should expect to be stretched in every area of your faith walk. The way you think, how far in advance you can reach the peak of your understanding, and how your patience will be tested far more than anything else is all a major set up for GOD to shift you into the best position of your life.

Proverbs 3:6 leads us to act, "In all thy ways acknowledge him, and he shall direct thy paths."

You have to get to a point in your walk of faith that nothing or no one stops you, limits you, pressures you, distracts you, sways you, persuades, or pushes you from remaining focused on what pleases the One True GOD we serve.

Chapter 7
The Faith Cycle

The Faith cycle has been revealed to me while reading from
Romans 1:17 (AMP)

"For in the gospel the righteousness of God is revealed, both springing from faith and leading to faith [disclosed in a way that awakens more faith]. As it is written and forever remains written, "The just and upright shall live by faith."

The Faith Cycle is assembled as a series of lessons and incidents that turn into victories of believing in strengths GOD has given you, which promotes maturity.

As maturity increases, increase attracts new challenges and encounters, and those challenges and encounters lead your determinations into conquering results. They are all geared by faith and the use of having the faith that ultimately works for you.

Sometimes, a question will present itself as if to glimpse all the steps I should take. I have often explained to GOD that I didn't want to know. For me to know gives me an out not to utilize the gift of His faith. Why? I would try to skip the exercises needed to be learned and not rely on Him through such faith and obedience required to attain the best purposeful outcome. I'd rather endure these encounters to learn more about myself, through GOD's eyes. This is very extreme to say. However, sometimes the best way to learn is to endure through forced maturity.

Being too comfortable and content can be dangerous to your growth, as it leads to slothfulness.

And sometimes, it is better to learn the different stages of your growth development than skipping the natural stages of that growth. This is called maturity.

I understand it this way. My true reward is not only getting to the promise; it is the process by which I go.

What do I mean by that?

The blessing is not only getting to the promise; it has

to do with having the ability to absorb the many lessons needed to mature into your promise (i.e., next stage, development, dimension, or realm). After I arrived at my promise, I am now expected to withstand another set of challenges REQUIRED to maintain that matured stage I've earned within the process. Think of faith like a stepping ladder. To excel to the next level, you must step up, seeing higher than before. Having gained a new perspective as you advance each earned step, you must maintain and improve on the next level.

So, when GOD shares with me why He did, what He did, and how He did it, I would have gained a greater appreciation for the process because I learned the lessons needed to get to my promise.

And that, my friends, is the "The Faith Cycle."

Q: What's the point of faith if we already know what will happen next, and why would GOD want us to seek Him in everything we do before we do it?

A: The entire chapter of **Psalm 37** WOW! Meditate on this passage when you feel like you are a welcome mat for other peoples' unresolved issues. After you finish reading and savoring every word, pay attention to how you've become clothed in victory. Notice how the Spirit of the Lord will resurrect your innermost strength. Shift your mindset and EMBRACE that there is No Such Thing or Person capable of prohibiting your progression of reaching the dimension of faith GOD requires of you. You have always been equipped and empowered before the foundations of the world. Congratulations, you've ascended beyond that circumstance. Now, Keep Going!

Chapter 8
When It's Your Turn

It is now your turn to be who God called you to be. Forget about everything else that you thought you knew about yourself because God has a unique way of recreating your entire makeup from the one you used to know. Even to the point where it's being remade by the way you think. Have you ever reached a place in your life where nothing is normal; everything you do and feel requires REAL Faith? Yes. It's that Amplified version of Romans 12:2 that has a hold of you. You have been released and set free from the faithless clutter you've built up over the years, trying to figure out who you are. But after you finally realize that you've entrapped yourself by hoarding your ambitions, forcing you to become tangled in a world without hearing much of the true Voice of GOD for yourself.

Q: Have you ever faced a challenge you haven't prepared for, and suddenly fear cloud your judgment?

Have you ever considered the transition toward bigger and greater encounters, having learned and gained valuable experiences and exposures with GOD to be too much to bear during mid-stride?

Have you ever thought that there seems to be nothing more you could do to improve what you are involved in because of thinking you're in over your head in the responsibility of faith?

A: If your answer is Yes, Good! You exactly are where God wants you to be. *James 1:2-4 (VOICE) "Don't run from tests and hardships, brothers and sisters. As difficult as they are, you will ultimately find joy in them; if you embrace them, your faith will blossom under pressure and teach you true patience as you endure. And true patience brought on by endurance will equip you to complete the long journey and cross the finish line—mature, complete, and wanting nothing."*

Fear of the "unknown" causes us to limit our progressive ability to look beyond the mask of defeat. Instead, we should walk through those uncertain and unsure areas in our lives. Raise your chin, look towards the hills from which cometh your help *(Psalm 121:1)* and stand firm in your faith amidst knowing every step and detail. This is what applying Faith is all about.

It wasn't until I established a right relationship with God that I recognized the progressive changes He's made through me.

You will no longer linger or mosey on everyday projects-wandering aimlessly, looking for opportunities to keep busy. You are to fill in the gaps of lacking a sense of divine purpose. As a young man, I would look for meaningless projects to keep my mind occupied, which I thought were purposeful. There were some assignments I knew were fruit-bearing, purposeful gifts for the Kingdom. However, sometimes I wasn't ready to fully understand the next assignment or thought of the tasks as difficult and too complicated to complete.

Before you can fully walk in the God-given purpose He has planned for you, there will be a set of exercising challenges you must conquer before you get to your promise. Even during this journey, there will be eye-opening, faith-building factors that will change the trajectory of your perception regarding your previous walk with Him. When the Gates of Heaven are open to you, everything may seem chaotic around you. That's because the world's process of things no longer has a grip on your life now you're in the right hands. What is on the other side of Chaos? Tranquility & Peace! Where there is shelter, peace resides.

Our life is not our own. You never know who prayed for a miracle or an angel to show up with an answer disguised as you.

Everything we've been given and blessed to have, we are only stewards of. We are held accountable for saying, thinking, and using what we have been entrusted with. Recognize and understand that we have been gifted and anointed to be a blessing for others.

Read Psalm 91:1-16, and I pray that the spectrum of your understanding will change how you are covered from Heaven on Earth. Although storms may rage on the outside, there is a peace deep within. Which will you choose to acknowledge?

Chapter 9
The Process of Faith

The standards for true believers are established within the Trust Processes of Faith. The development of your faith through Christ sheds light on Kingdom Living. Kingdom Living is about taking action through the processes of faith, operating in your authority as a Kingdom Citizen, and fully understanding your purpose while using your gifts and talents through Christ.

All that, just so you can confidently proclaim, *"Let your light shine before men in such a way that they may see your good deeds and moral excellence, and [recognize and honor and] glory your father who is in Heaven."* Matthew 5:16 AMP

There comes a time that God will portion you to sample sections of your faith as an exercise to build/increase your faith to a higher standard. Remember the faith ladder example I mentioned earlier? All in all, your standards are noticeably advanced to you because GOD's got you doing it

It is not enough to only believe that Christ was raised from the dead to have the true [get this keyword] "*knowledge*" of faith. The word Knowledge is defined as facts, information, and skills acquired by a person through experience or education; the theoretical or practical understanding of a subject.

So, when GOD shares with me why He did, what He did, and how He did it, I would gain a greater appreciation for the process because I learned the lessons needed to get to my promise.

I'll coin this as "The Faith Cycle" The Faith cycle has been revealed to me while reading from Romans 1:17 (AMP)

"For in the gospel the righteousness of God is revealed, both springing from faith and leading to faith [disclosed in a way that awakens more faith]. As it is written and forever remains written, "The just and upright shall live by faith."

The Faith cycle is assembled as a series of lessons and incidents that turn into victories of believing in strengths

GOD has given you, which promotes maturity. As maturity increases, increase attracts new challenges and encounters, and those challenges and encounters lead your determinations into conquering results. They are all geared by faith and the use of having the faith that ultimately works for you.

He believes that you can get through the experience with high flying colors because you'll believe that you can. Your spoken declarations will begin to leap higher than you thought. You've begun to realize that there was never a ceiling to limit your talent and abilities. You've taken into careful consideration the very purpose you were meant to thrive here on Earth and understand that the limits you've placed over yourself no longer apply. You're having eureka moments where life is not ahead of you any longer.

As you know, life is competing for a position to take the lead, and because we as believers live by faith, we are not threatened with what the world's standards are. You Now Have a KINGDOM MINDSET and have begun to walk as Kings and Queens do. The steps that you take are very precise in spirit and are displayed in truth daily.

You've become an overcomer!

A life worth living by faith requires one to have an overcoming mindset.

What does authority mean to you?

What does dominion mean to you?

What will you do to apply what you've learned to your everyday life?

Chapter 10
Expectancy

To expect great things, you must have the innate ability to shift your mindset. Adjusting your mindset means to train your mind to shift in faith toward the promise. This could mean the ideas you have regarding yourself, the situation or circumstance you're in, a negative lie you told yourself, or anything outside of what the Word of God says you are. Never and I mean never speak nor think in your heart against yourself in any other direction that does not lead to progression. Your expectation of greater things with the right action plan, including intentional application, is a direct set up for great things to manifest in your life.

Growth in the spirit requires a process. The process of being molded into greatness is strenuous. However, there are properties of maturity we must embrace. Maturity is vital and the most integral tool used in GOD's strategies to fix, break, shatter, restore, improve, renew, replace and construct a diverse system of awareness within us that only He can do.

Once you are fully operating in His will, you must acknowledge that He will and can use whatever situation, circumstance, person, or thing to reveal, teach, instruct and command anything deemed sufficient for His intended purposes. Remember that you are in God's hands, and that is the best place for you to be in, especially while you are operating in obedience.

Isaiah 55:8

"For my thoughts are not your thoughts; neither are your ways my ways says the Lord."

Isaiah 55:9 KJV

"For as the heavens are higher than the Earth, so are my ways higher than your ways, and my thoughts than your thoughts."

Proverbs 23:26 NIV

"My son, give me your heart and let your eyes delight in my ways."

Therefore, acknowledge the ways of the Lord regardless of understanding. Take courage and obey with joy, and watch your joy be increased through active obedience.

Chapter 11
Repent, Release & Repeat

Knowing when to repent is just as important as breathing. There are passages in the bible describing what happens when turning from bondage to the grace of faith through repentance.

2 Corinthians 3:16-18 states, "But whenever anyone turns to the LORD, the veil is taken away. Now the LORD is the Spirit, and where the Spirit of the LORD is, there is freedom. And we all, who with unveiled faces contemplate the LORD's glory, are being transformed into His image with ever-increasing glory, which comes from the LORD, who is the Spirit."

There are passages in the bible describing what

happens when turning from bondage to the grace of faith through repentance.

As believers, if we don't know that this is a fundamental principle, we'll remain entrapped by not consistently repenting. The use and repetition of Repent, Release, Repeat is vital to one's growth as a believer because the practical application keeps us rooted and aligned with the statutes of a fruitful spirit (See Galatians 5:22-26). Unfortunately, some of us tend to think we don't struggle with things that will grow inwardly to harm us. Contrarily, because we've overlooked the matter, that "thing" seems to have grown overnight like mold or fungi, feeding away on the purity we've established by long-suffering faith.

Don't allow another moment to slip by without releasing what isn't right within you. If you are unsure that there may be something wrong, you can always consult the Holy Spirit to show you what those things are.

Snap out of thinking you are too busy to repent. If that's your way of thinking, then your camp may be tainted. Expecting to feel convicted to repent is the wrong idea.

Look at Acts 26:20: To repent is a result of a change of mind that results in a change of action. Our actions of repentance are wrong because we've been taught wrong.

Look at Acts 17:30...

You ever wonder why you feel unproductive, yet you have all the tools, resources, and knowledge to get the job done? That's because you may need to find out what those things are in your life that are blocking your progress. Start by asking the Holy Spirit what the blockage is so you may purge by repentance and repent as often as possible. The bible says that we are to pray without ceasing. This goes for repenting as well.

"Rejoice always and delight in your faith; <u>be unceasing and persistent in prayer; in every situation [no matter what the circumstances]</u> be thankful and continually give thanks to GOD; for this is the will of GOD for you in Christ Jesus. Do not quench [subdue, or be unresponsive to the working and guidance of] the [Holy] Spirit. Do not scorn or reject gifts of prophecy or prophecies [spoken revelations--words of instruction or exhortation or warning]. But test all things carefully [so you can recognize what is good]. Hold firmly to that which is good. Abstain from every form of evil [withdraw and keep away from it]. Now may the GOD of peace Himself sanctify you through and through [that is, separate you from profane and vulgar things, make you pure and whole and undamaged--consecrated to Him-- set apart for His purpose]; and may your spirit and soul and body be kept complete and [be found] blameless at the coming of our Lord Jesus Christ." 1

THESSALONIANS 5:16-23 AMP

One major player in practical application to use is to die daily to ourselves. Dying daily to ourselves allows us to become more receptive to what GOD is saying, and it helps us rid of any selfish characteristics we may have hidden in our hearts. Lay yourself before GOD and repent daily, asking GOD to relieve you from yourself or anything that would exalt itself before Him. Invite Adonai Yeshua's spirit into your heart. Declare in spirit what you are expecting, according to GOD's will.

Chapter 12
Wandering in the Past is a Trap

Don't allow your fears of the past to control your future. The past comes with many forms, such as shadows, shame, embarrassment, misfortune, mistakes, fake self-image, total disregard of right-doing and decision-making, etc. On the contrary, glancing in the past can also teach about your growth, maturity, and the directions you've taken, the advancement of discretion, and learned behaviors you can use to re-evaluate yourself moving forward.

There is a greater purpose ahead of you, so you must ignore the negative shadows that lie behind you. The shadows of your past will always follow you because it's an important part of your history. However, the negative details of your past should not define who you have become. So, stand in the light of God's word and allow His light to shine before you.

Prayer Invitation

Pray a prayer that rebukes fear, uncertainty, doubt, etc.

I want to take a few moments to open the floodgates of Heaven. This is an open invitation to fully allow the Holy Spirit to invade the fullness of your heart. Seek Him out in your Eden place, prayer space, secret closet, etc. No matter where you are. If you're driving, listening to this audiobook, pull over and give him your whole heart. Ask the Holy Spirit to come in and remove any and everything that is unfruitful within you. Ask the Holy Spirit to thoroughly clean and breakdown your vessel in removing all impurities found inside your heart and to restore everything of Christ's spirit that should be in the place of those voids back to God's original setting. Ask for His anointing and authority to reveal revelations, shower down wisdom and understanding, to know and apply what has been given your heart. Release yourself from the driver's seat and ask Christ to take full control to do, walk, and speak His will. IN Yeshua's name, Amen!

Your life will change as you continue to make yourself available to be taught and guided by His presence through His word.

Citations

https://blogjob.com/experiencingGod/tag/crisis-of-belief/
page 2 of Hidden Figures

https://www.biblesprout.com/articles/christian-life/steps-for-dealing-with-doubt/

Biblical References

Psalms 23:16 - **Intro**

II Timothy 1:7

Philippians 14:13 - **Hidden Figures**

Romans 8:28

John 14:6

James 2:26

Proverbs 23:15-16

Ephesians 3:20

I Corinthians 15:57

I Corinthians 10:13 - **Distractions**

Matthew 11:28-30

Psalm 34:8 - **Knock, Knock**

Romans 10:9 - **Difference Makers**

Romans 12:2

Matthew 14:22-32

Jeremiah 29:11

II Timothy 1:7

Luke 5 - **Faith That Stretches Your Strength**

I Peter 2:9

Proverbs 3:6

Romans 1:17 - **The Faith Cycle**

Psalms 37

Romans 12:2 - **When It's Your Turn**

James 1:2-4

Psalms 121:1

Psalms 91:1-16

Matthew 5:16 - **The Process of Faith**

Romans 1:17

Isaiah 55:8-9 - **Expectancy**

Proverbs 23:26

II Corinthians 3:16-18 - **Repent, Release & Repeat**

Galatians 5:22-26

Acts 26:20

Acts 17:30

I Thessalonians 5:16-23

About the Author

Daniel Lee is an extraordinary Spiritual Confidence Mentor, helping to build the confidence of men by breaking barriers of fear and leading them to God's purpose for their lives.

With over 15 years of experience in prophetic miming and 18 years in healthcare & project management, Daniel Lee has realized why God wanted to combine his gifts and talents together and use him as His vessel. Daniel has taken a moment to write about his faith journey. Though that journey has not been easy,

Daniel found that his faith increased after conquering doubt, fear, and disbelief. This has wholeheartedly catapulted His relationship with Yeshua.

Daniel is the co-founder of Affirm Me Apparel, a kingdom clothing brand that relays affirmations from God that confirms You Are Who God Says You Are.

Daniel lives in Atlanta, Georgia with his wife, LaToya Sharee, teaching and ministering the word of God daily within their online ministry and Discipleship Academy. They are the proud parents of Blake and Blair McLeod.

Visit www.iamdaniellee.com to download your free guide "5 Secrets to Overcoming Fear" and get more information about the vision for ministry and business endeavors.

Associations

www.joyinternationalministries.org

www.emunahdiscipleshipacademy.com

www.affirmmeapparel.com

www.ingramcontent.com/pod-product-compliance
Lightning Source LLC
Chambersburg PA
CBHW030225170426
43194CB00007BA/867